Ela Area Public Library District

275 Mohawk Trail, Lake Zurich, IL 60047
(847) 438-3433
www.eapl.org

W9-BCP-073

OCT – – 2019

FASHION FIGURES

KATE HUDSON

FASHIONABLE

FITNESS CO-FOUNDER

Jessica Rusick

Checkerboard
Library

An Imprint of Abdo Publishing
abdobooks.com

abdobooks.com

Published by Abdo Publishing, a division of ABDO, PO Box 398166, Minneapolis, Minnesota 55439.
Copyright © 2020 by Abdo Consulting Group, Inc. International copyrights reserved in all countries.
No part of this book may be reproduced in any form without written permission from the publisher.
Checkerboard Library™ is a trademark and logo of Abdo Publishing.

Printed in the United States of America, North Mankato, Minnesota
052019
092019

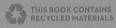
THIS BOOK CONTAINS
RECYCLED MATERIALS

Design: Aruna Rangarajan, Mighty Media, Inc.
Production: Mighty Media, Inc.
Editor: Rebecca Felix
Design Elements: Shutterstock Images
Cover Photograph: Shutterstock Images
Interior Photographs: AP Images, pp. 15, 23, 25, 29 (left, center); Getty Images, pp. 5, 17, 19, 21; Seth
Poppel/Yearbook Library, p. 7; Shutterstock Images, pp. 9, 11, 13, 27, 28 (left, top, bottom), 29 (right)

Library of Congress Control Number: 2018966452

Publisher's Cataloging-in-Publication Data

Names: Rusick, Jessica, author.
Title: Kate Hudson: fashionable fitness co-founder / by Jessica Rusick
Other title: Fashionable fitness co-founder
Description: Minneapolis, Minnesota : Abdo Publishing, 2020 | Series: Fashion figures | Includes online
    resources and index.
Identifiers: ISBN 9781532119514 (lib. bdg.) | ISBN 9781532173974 (ebook)
Subjects: LCSH: Hudson, Kate, 1979- --Juvenile literature. | Fashion designers--United States--Biography--
    Juvenile literature. | Motion picture actors and actresses--Biography--Juvenile literature. | Women
    authors, American--Biography--Juvenile literature. | Women entrepreneurs--Biography--Juvenile
    literature.
Classification: DDC 746.920922 [B]--dc23

CONTENTS

Fashion & Fitness Icon 4

Acting & Athletics 6

Film, Fame & Family 8

A New Focus 10

The Face of Fabletics 14

Fashion for All.. 16

First Sales & Flops.. 18

Fabletics Finds Its Footing................................... 20

#Fitspo 22

Future & Fashion.. 26

Timeline 28

Glossary 30

Online Resources 31

Index.. 32

FASHION & FITNESS ICON

Kate Hudson is an actor and fashion **entrepreneur**. She helped develop the popular brand Fabletics. Fabletics makes women's athletic clothing.

Hudson co-founded Fabletics in 2013. She helps run the business. She also models clothing. Hudson helped Fabletics become successful after the company faced an unsure start. Now, the company has millions of fans worldwide.

Hudson believes fitness can be fashionable and fun. Her brand is known for its colorful, simple clothing. Fabletics also takes an **inclusive** approach to fitness. The company's **motto** is "Live Your Passion." It aims to inspire women to achieve their fitness goals.

As a child, Hudson was creative and active. But she would not join the fashion world until later in her career. Before becoming a fashion and fitness icon, Hudson first became a movie star!

Hudson's Fabletics brand makes athletic wear for a healthy, active lifestyle.

ACTING & ATHLETICS

Kate Garry Hudson was born on April 19, 1979, in Los Angeles, California. Her mother is actor Goldie Hawn. Her father is musician Bill Hudson. Kate's parents divorced when she was 18 months old. Goldie began dating actor Kurt Russell. He raised Kate. Kate has an older brother, two half-**siblings**, and one stepbrother.

Kate liked to sing, act, and dance from an early age. She took ballet from ages 3 to 14. She says ballet taught her how to stay healthy. Kate also played sports. She was a soccer player. Kate's early love of fitness would one day help her become a fashion icon!

As a teen, Kate remained interested in sports and acting. While in high school, she was cast in her first acting role. She was on an episode of the TV show *Party of Five* in 1996. Kate graduated high school in 1997. She then began **auditioning** for movie roles.

IN HER OWN WORDS

"I've lived in activewear my entire life."
—Kate Hudson

Kate (*top, middle*) with soccer teammates during her sophomore year of high school

Kate as a high school sophomore, acting in the play *Man of La Mancha*

FILM, FAME & FAMILY

Auditioning for movies was more **frustrating** than Hudson expected. She felt casting directors were more interested in her looks and voice than in her acting skills. But Hudson kept trying.

Her hard work paid off! Hudson earned several small roles on TV shows and movies over the next four years. But it was a lead role in the movie *Almost Famous* that would make her a star.

At first, Hudson was cast in a smaller role in *Almost Famous*. But before filming began, the original leading actress dropped out of the movie. The film's director recast Hudson as the leading actress!

Almost Famous was released in 2000. Hudson won a 2001 Best Supporting Actress Golden Globe award for the film. Soon, she was offered more movie roles. She became a movie star.

As Hudson's career took off, her personal life was also changing. In 2000, she married musician Chris Robinson. They had a son, Ryder, in 2004. The couple divorced in 2006. Then in 2011, Hudson

Hudson with (*from left*) son Ryder, mother Hawn, and stepdad Russell

and her boyfriend, Matt Bellamy, had a son named Bingham. The couple split up in 2014.

Hudson found it hard to spend time away from her sons while filming movies. She wanted to take fewer acting roles. She started to think of new projects that would keep her close to her family.

A NEW FOCUS

As Hudson thought about a new career direction in 2013, her mind went to fashion. Many stars are involved in successful fashion lines. Hudson thought she could be one of them.

On the **red carpet**, Hudson often wore fancy dresses. When people in the fashion world heard Hudson wanted to design clothes, they thought she meant dresses. But Hudson wanted to make clothing closer to her everyday style.

Fitness had remained important to Hudson as an adult. Off the red carpet, she often wore athleisure clothing. The word *athleisure* is a blend of "athletic" and "leisure." Athleisure clothing is designed for exercise but is comfortable and fashionable enough to be worn anywhere. It includes leggings, yoga pants, and sweatshirts.

Hudson wore athleisure clothing when she exercised, took her kids to school, and more. And she was not alone! Hudson's style was part of an emerging fashion trend.

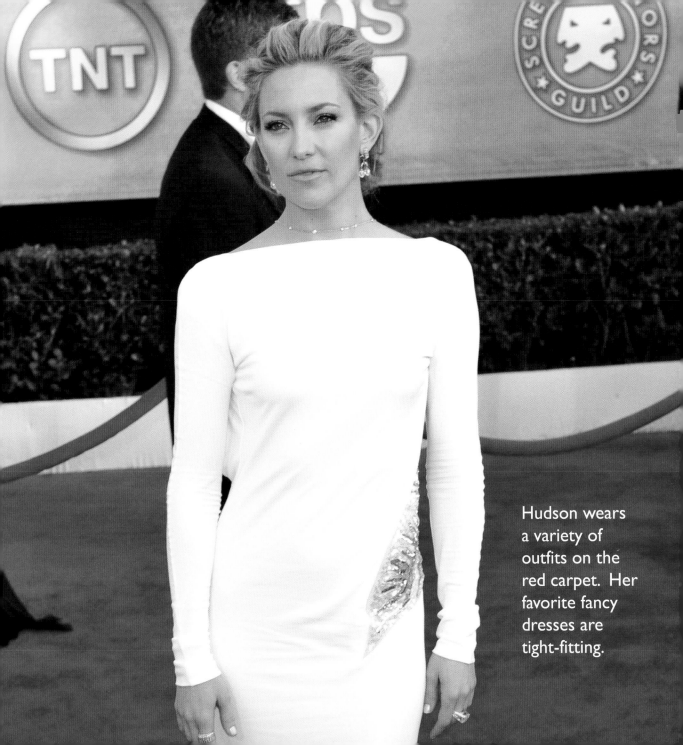

Hudson wears a variety of outfits on the red carpet. Her favorite fancy dresses are tight-fitting.

In the past, it was not fashionable to wear athletic clothing outside the gym. But in the 2010s, it became popular to wear athleisure clothing anywhere and everywhere. Today, more people wear athleisure clothing than ever before. Athleisure clothing sales rose by more than $100 billion between 2007 and 2016.

Athleisure clothing is popular because it is comfortable and **durable**. It stays wrinkle-free and odor-free longer than regular clothing does. This is because athleisure clothing is made from high-tech fabrics, such as **spandex**.

Fashion experts say the popularity of athleisure wear represents a shift in how Americans live. More people are interested in leading active **lifestyles**. The trend also shows that people want clothing items that can serve multiple purposes.

Clothing brands including Lululemon, Nike, and Athleta sold athleisure clothing. But Hudson

FASHION FACT

In past centuries, women's athletic clothing was often stiff and uncomfortable. This changed in the late 1800s, when women sought more comfortable clothing for riding bikes and playing tennis.

Fabletics has created increased competition for more expensive athletic clothing brand Lululemon in recent years.

believed these brands' clothing was too expensive. A pair of Lululemon yoga pants often cost more than $100.

Hudson knew many people might want athleisure clothing but not be able to afford those prices. She believed affordable athletic wear would be a big hit with consumers. Hudson had found her next project. She wanted to create a fitness clothing line!

THE FACE OF FABLETICS

Fashion **entrepreneurs** Don Ressler and Adam Goldenberg heard Hudson was interested in starting a fashion line. In July 2013, they approached Hudson with an idea.

Ressler and Goldenberg had just started a company called Fabletics that would sell fitness clothing online. Like Hudson, they saw the need for affordable athleisure wear. They asked Hudson if she wanted to join Fabletics as a co-founder.

The two men felt Hudson was the perfect fit as co-founder. They knew she lived an active **lifestyle** and wore athleisure clothing.

Ressler and Goldenberg also believed Hudson had a friendly personality. They felt this, as well as Hudson's popularity as a movie star, would help

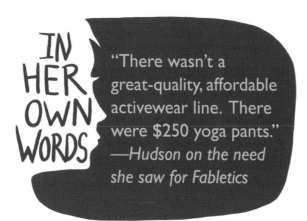

IN HER OWN WORDS

"There wasn't a great-quality, affordable activewear line. There were $250 yoga pants." —Hudson on the need she saw for Fabletics

As the face of Fabletics, Hudson represented the brand in interviews and at media events.

the company connect to customers. In addition to becoming a co-founder, Hudson became the face of Fabletics. She would model the brand's clothing and appear in its commercials and print advertisements.

FASHION FOR ALL

Hudson also felt her partnership with Fabletics was a great fit. She believed she could help the company take a fun approach to promoting fitness. She wanted to help women look stylish and achieve their personal fitness goals.

Hudson knew exercising is **stressful** for some women. This is because fitness brands often pressure women to look a certain way. Hudson did not want her brand to send this message.

Most athleisure clothing at the time was black or gray and expensive. Hudson wanted to make it fashionable and affordable for women to wear colorful items too. Fabletics would go beyond blacks and grays to make items in bright colors and prints. These vibrant designs became part of the brand's **signature** style.

Hudson gave input on Fabletics items as they were created. She also helped form the company's budgets and social media plan. A few months after Hudson joined, Fabletics was ready to launch.

Hudson exercised and socialized with women in California during a Fabletics event in 2014.

FIRST SALES & FLOPS

In October 2013, Fabletics launched its first line of clothes. The first product it sold was leggings. The line later included tank tops, sports bras, and more. Fabletics released new designs every month. That way, customers would check back often to see what was new. Hudson felt this set her clothing company apart from others.

Hudson was also proud of Fabletics' membership program. Customers could pay $50 a month for a VIP membership. This allowed them to buy the brand's clothes at lower prices than non-members.

Members gave Fabletics their banking information when signing up. They could choose not to pay $50 during months when they didn't want to buy anything. But they had to enter this decision in their account by the fifth day of that month to avoid getting charged.

Hudson thought this system was cutting-edge. Members did not. Many said the Fabletics website did not make it clear that signing up meant a monthly charge. Some members felt tricked and were angry.

Fabletics also sells exercise equipment and accessories, such as yoga mats and towels.

With customers already upset about membership confusion, Fabletics ran into another blunder. Its clothing was selling out too quickly. Many items on the website were always out of stock. Some consumers started to wonder if Fabletics was a scam.

FABLETICS FINDS ITS FOOTING

Hudson wanted to turn consumer opinions of Fabletics around. She led an effort over the next three years to fix communication between the company and its customers. This effort included updating the Fabletics website to better explain the monthly membership.

Another website update focused on solving the problem of selling out of items. Fabletics added a Style Quiz that popped up when new customers visited the website. The quiz asked customers about their workout habits, favorite colors, and what clothing sizes they wear.

The quiz data helped Fabletics estimate how much clothing to make and in what sizes and colors. Hudson also looked at sales numbers to see which items were most popular. This helped Fabletics determine which designs to make more of.

By 2016, Hudson's ideas for changing consumer opinions of Fabletics worked! Customer complaints went down and sales increased. After a rocky start, Hudson's brand had found its footing.

Fabletics started to open stores across the United States in 2015. Hudson went to one of the first store openings in New Jersey.

#FITSPO

As Fabletics took off, Hudson became a fitness inspiration. She often posted photos and videos of her workouts on Instagram, where she had more than 9 million followers!

Hudson wore Fabletics clothes in these posts. In some posts, she was on a **Pilates** machine. Other times, she was doing yoga or hiking. No matter the workout, Hudson liked to exercise outdoors.

Fans often shared Hudson's posts with the label #fitspo. This word is a blend of "fitness" and "inspiration." But Hudson's fans also inspired her. Some fans posted about their fitness goals using #Fabletics or #MyFabletics. Hudson loved looking through these posts and seeing women working to achieve their personal bests.

Fabletics members also inspired Hudson to write books. She was impressed by the way Fabletics members helped and supported one another. Many shared fitness and life advice in online forums. Hudson wanted to do the same by sharing her own advice.

Hudson's brother Oliver Hudson is the spokesperson for Fabletics' menswear line, FL2. The line debuted in 2015.

In 2016, Hudson published her first book, *Pretty Happy*. It includes her tips on living a happy and healthy life. One topic in the book is **meditation**. Hudson's mother told her to try it when Hudson was going through a hard time in her life. Now meditation is part of Hudson's wellness routine.

Pretty Happy became a best seller. In 2017, Hudson published a second book, *Pretty Fun*. In this book, she shares her favorite healthy recipes and gives tips on throwing fun, meaningful gatherings.

Hudson has also remained interested and involved in making films. In 2016, she directed and filmed a 30-second Fabletics commercial on her smartphone. That same year, she starred in the movie *Deepwater Horizon* alongside her stepdad, Russell. Although she still acts, Hudson now spends more time working on Fabletics than she does in Hollywood.

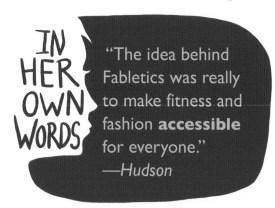

IN HER OWN WORDS

"The idea behind Fabletics was really to make fitness and fashion **accessible** for everyone."
—*Hudson*

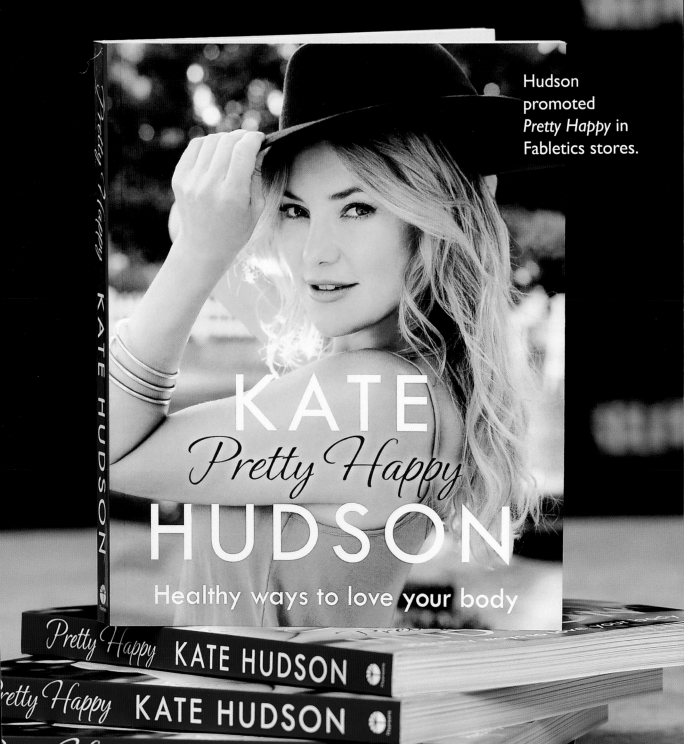

KATE
Pretty Happy
HUDSON

Healthy ways to love **your** body

Pretty Happy **KATE HUDSON**

Pretty Happy **KATE HUDSON**

Hudson promoted *Pretty Happy* in Fabletics stores.

FUTURE & FASHION

Fabletics continues to follow Hudson's mission to make affordable athleisure wear **accessible** for all women. In 2017, the company began offering clothing in more sizes, from XXS to 3X.

Fabletics continues to grow in other ways too. In 2017, it had more than 1.2 million members and made $250 million. In 2018, Fabletics opened a store in the United Kingdom. It plans to open 75 stores in the United States and around the world in coming years.

Hudson's family also grew in 2018. On October 2, Hudson and her boyfriend, Danny Fujikawa, welcomed a daughter named Rani.

Today, Hudson's career goals are to **empower** women. She was one of 300 Hollywood stars who started the Time's Up movement in 2018. This movement addresses women's equality in the workplace.

Hudson continues to inspire women with her **lifestyle** and brand. Her love for fitness and fashion has helped many women achieve their goals and feel good while doing so!

Hudson and
boyfriend Danny
Fujikawa in 2018

TIMELINE

Hudson has a son, Ryder, with husband Chris Robinson.

Hudson lands her first acting role on the TV show *Party of Five*.

Hudson has a son, Bingham, with boyfriend Matt Bellamy.

1996

2004

2011

1979

2000

2010s

Kate's breakout film, *Almost Famous*, is released.

Athleisure clothing becomes a fashion trend in the United States.

Kate Garry Hudson is born on April 19 in Los Angeles, California.

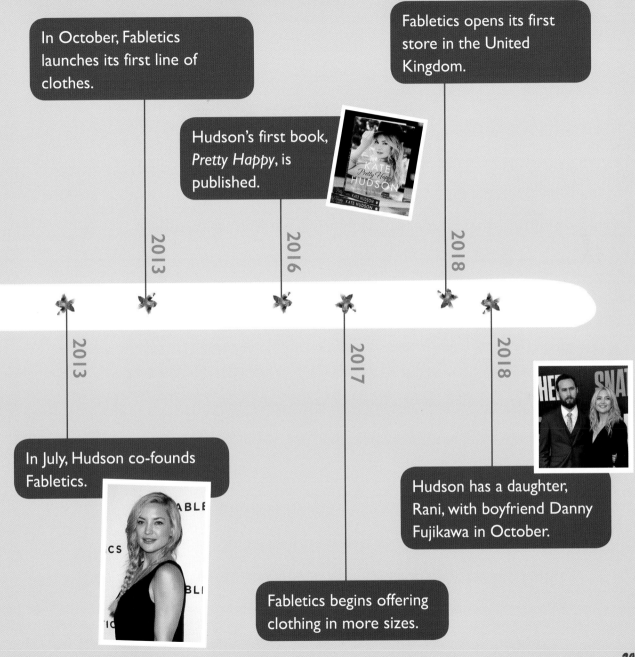

In October, Fabletics launches its first line of clothes.

Hudson's first book, *Pretty Happy*, is published.

Fabletics opens its first store in the United Kingdom.

2013

2016

2018

2013

2017

2018

In July, Hudson co-founds Fabletics.

Fabletics begins offering clothing in more sizes.

Hudson has a daughter, Rani, with boyfriend Danny Fujikawa in October.

GLOSSARY

accessible—being within reach.

audition—to give a trial performance showcasing personal talent as a musician, a singer, a dancer, or an actor.

durable—able to exist for a long time without weakening.

empower—to promote or influence someone becoming stronger and more confident, especially in taking control of their life and claiming their rights.

entrepreneur—one who organizes, manages, and accepts the risks of a business or an enterprise.

frustrating—causing feelings of anger or annoyance.

inclusive—welcoming to everyone.

lifestyle—the way a being, group, or society lives.

meditation—the act of thinking deeply and quietly.

motto—a word or sentence that describes a guiding principle.

Pilates—a type of exercise that is usually performed on a floor mat and meant to improve flexibility and stability.

red carpet—a long, narrow red carpet placed on the ground for important or famous people to walk on when arriving at an event.

sibling—a brother or a sister.

signature—something that sets apart or identifies an individual, group, or company.

spandex—any of various stretchy textile fibers.

stressful—full of or causing strain or pressure.

ONLINE RESOURCES

Booklinks
NONFICTION NETWORK
FREE! ONLINE NONFICTION RESOURCES

To learn more about Kate Hudson, please visit **abdobooklinks.com** or scan this QR code. These links are routinely monitored and updated to provide the most current information available.

INDEX

acting career, 4, 6, 8, 9, 10, 24
advertising, 15, 24
Almost Famous, 8
athleisure, 10, 12, 13, 14, 16, 26
Athleta, 12, 13
awards, 8

Bellamy, Matt, 8, 9
books, 22, 24

California, 6, 24, 26

Deepwater Horizon, 24

education, 6

Fabletics
  membership, 18, 19, 20, 22, 26
  sales, 18, 20, 26
  social media, 16, 22
  website, 18, 19, 20
family, 6, 8, 9, 24, 26
Fujikawa, Danny, 26

Goldenberg, Adam, 14, 15

Hawn, Goldie, 6, 24
health, 6, 24
Hudson, Bill, 6

Lululemon, 12, 13

Nike, 12, 13

Party of Five, 6
personal style, 10, 14
Pretty Fun, 24
Pretty Happy, 24

Ressler, Don, 14, 15
Robinson, Chris, 8
Russell, Kurt, 6, 24

sports, 6, 10, 16, 18, 22

Time's Up movement, 26